The Daisies Are Still Free

THE DAISIES ARE STILL FREE

Patricia Wilson

THE UPPER ROOM

The Daisies Are Still Free

Copyright © 1982 The Upper Room. All rights reserved. No part of this book may be reproduced in any manner whatsoever without written permission of the publisher except in brief quotations embodied in critical articles or reviews. For information address The Upper Room, 1908 Grand Avenue, P. O. Box 189, Nashville, Tennessee 37202-0189.

"I'd Pick More Daisies" is reprinted by permission from the *Christian Athlete* magazine (Oct., 1974), official publication of the Fellowship of Christian Athletes and is used by permission of the magazine.

Scripture quotations are from the Revised Standard Version of the Bible, copyrighted 1946, 1952 and © 1971 by the Division of Christian Education, National Council of Churches of Christ in the United States of America, and are used by permission.

Book Design: Harriette Bateman
Cover Photo by John Netherton
First printing: May 1982 (7)
Second Printing: February 1984 (7)
Library of Congress Catalog Card Number: 82-50305
ISBN: 0-8358-0444-5
Printed in the United States of America

*For my mother,
who has
always known
that the
daisies
are free*

Contents

Foreword by George Anderson 9
Preface 11
1. Hurray for the Red X's! 15
2. Under the Mattress 21
3. The Singing Joy 29
4. Grab at a Chance 35
5. Pruning the Rosebushes 43
6. Chocolate Sundae Heaven 51
7. There's No Such Thing as a Dragon 59
8. The Great, Gray Bird 65
9. Living in the Now 73
10. "Ladybird, Ladybird, Fly Away Home" 79
11. An Exercise in Sole Touching 87
12. Dance to My Own Song 93
13. Let's Run Away from Home! 99
14. The Daisies Are Still Free 105

Foreword

The Daisies Are Still Free is written by one whom I once described as being an eclectic person with a grasp of life that permitted the designing of a lifestyle from the best that came her way.

In the brochure that was written, the typesetter had used the word *electric* instead of *eclectic*—and that's not too far off for she is a real "live wire." Pat Wilson is as much at home building a cement fish pond or garden walk for her family as she is in the boardroom of the Ontario Government Department for which she works. In the entertainment and arts programs which she finds so challenging in her community, she is as much at home as in her church and faith commitments.

In these pages you will see yourself because she has the ability to lift the ordinary, everyday experiences and draw from them laughter, tears, pathos, and an awareness that, in all of our encounters, the One who created us is with us on the journey.

Pat has been associated with Faith at Work Canada

The Daisies Are Still Free

for a number of years as a board member. She has conducted workshops and seminars from coast to coast. It has been my pleasure to serve with her in conferences and to have her as a contributing writer to our publication *The Way*.

> GEORGE F. ANDERSON
> Executive Director,
> Faith at Work Canada

Preface

I'd Pick More Daisies

If I had my life to live over again, I'd try to make more mistakes next time. I would relax. I would limber up. I would be sillier than I have been this trip. I know of very few things I would take seriously. I would take more trips. I would climb more mountains, swim more rivers, and watch more sunsets. I would do more walking and looking. I would eat more ice cream and less beans. I would have more actual troubles and fewer imaginary ones. You see, I am one of those people who live prophylactically and sensibly and sanely hour after hour, day after day. Oh, I've had my moments and if I had it to do over again, I'd have more of them. In fact I'd try to have nothing else. Just moments, one after another, instead of living so many years ahead each day. I have been one of those people who never go anywhere without a thermometer, a hot water bottle, a gargle, a raincoat, aspirin, and a parachute. If I had it to do over again, I

The Daisies Are Still Free

would go places, do things and travel lighter than I have.

If I had my life to live over, I would start barefooted earlier in the spring and stay that way later in the fall. I would play hooky more. I wouldn't make such good grades except by accident. I would ride on more merry-go-rounds. I'd pick more daisies.

BROTHER JEREMIAH

I first read this little "poem" two years ago, just a few days after I got back from a Leadership Training Institute with Faith at Work. At the time, the words said exactly what I was feeling. I had come home convinced that I had my life to live over, and now I could do it with pizzazz!

In a burst of enthusiasm, I broke the poem down into bite-sized chunks and introduced the daisy-picker lifestyle to my Bible study/prayer group. The results were tremendous, better than I could have imagined. Lives changed, people were freed, and the daisies we picked seemed to sum up and express the freedom of life in Christ that had been so often before presented to us in dry words and phrases. When we finished the course, I decided that it had to be put into a book. There was something here for all of us.

I started the book many times, but somewhere the daisies eluded me and I couldn't honestly say that I

Preface

had it all worked out. Too many things seemed to interfere with what I had envisioned the daisy-picker lifestyle to be. I decided that perhaps it wasn't possible to pick the daisies in today's world—at least, not if you worked for a living or were tied down by responsibilities.

Over the past two years, my enthusiasm for the Christian life has waxed and waned as I have worked my way through various degrees of depression, grief, and anger. Occasionally, a daisy would surface. I would brush it off, smile sadly at what might have been, and bury it again.

I used the daisy-picker theme several times in workshops, and each time I thought I had a glimpse of what I could be. But a few days later, the cares of my little world would press in on me, and I would forget the daisies.

It's taken me all this time to discover that picking the daisies is not simply being a free spirit—free from cares, frustrations, worries, fears. Being a barefooted daisy picker is *being*, just being. The freedom is within, not without, and it's there for anyone. If I can find it, you can.

That's the reason I've finally written this book. Because the daisies are still free!

CHAPTER ONE

*"I'd like to make more
mistakes next time."*

Hurray
for the
Red X's!

Mistakes are wrong. Everyone knows that. Think back to your first arithmetic paper. Were the correct answers marked for special attention? No, it was the mistakes that were boldly marked with the red X.

My life sometimes seems like an arithmetic paper. No one notices the correct answers, but the mistakes are illuminated by flashing neon X's. I tend to measure my Christian life by the number of mistakes I've made: count the red X's and see what a good Christian I am. In the back of my mind is a small prophet of doom who gleefully tells me that Christians—real Christians—never make mistakes.

A red X must indicate that I didn't seek the Lord's will in the first place, or if I did, I didn't listen to the Lord's leading. No wonder I have concocted all sorts of methods to determine the Lord's will—little techniques guaranteed to prevent me from making mistakes.

The easiest method (and incidentally, the least satisfactory) is to play a quick game of "Bible Roulette."

Hurray for the Red X's!

The game is very simple: I offer the Lord my problem and the opportunity to tell me what to do. How? By opening my Bible at random and letting my eye fall on the first verse I see. If the Lord has played the game fairly, the verse will be pertinent to my question and will tell me exactly what to do.

In theory, it's a wonderful method. In practice, my eye usually falls on "And Fred begat Joe who begat Henry who begat. . . ." As I said, it can be very unsatisfactory.

Occasionally, the game works. There was a time when I was desperately praying for guidance regarding a trip to Florida. I opened the Bible, and my eye lighted on part of the Psalms: "They despised the pleasant land, having no faith in his promise" (Psalm 106:24). In February, Florida is indeed a promised land! I had faith in God's promises and went. I didn't make a mistake.

Then I discovered the method called "fleece setting." Actually, I didn't discover this method; Gideon did. He couldn't come to a decision about a battle, so he laid a sheepskin outside his tent and told the Lord that if in the morning the fleece were wet and the ground dry, he would do battle. The next morning, the fleece was wet and the ground was dry. But Gideon was more afraid of the red X than of the Lord. He put the fleece out again. The fleece would be dry, the ground would be wet, and Gideon would fight

The Daisies Are Still Free

the battle. They were, and even Gideon finally got the message.

My "fleeces" aren't quite as dramatic as Gideon's, but they're just as valid for me. I even put out a fleece for a husband. I didn't want to make a mistake there! Through a long chain of circumstances, I had a car that needed repairs, and I needed a strong man to make them.

My mother and I prayed about the car repairs, and Mom asked the Lord to send me the strong man I needed. I decided to add on my own request: "Make him someone special, Lord, and while you're at it, make him over six feet two inches and a Christian." That seemed to cover all bases. How could I go wrong?

A few days later, a friend doing a little matchmaking introduced me to Merv. We weren't immediately struck with each other, but we visited with our friends all afternoon. When it was time for me to leave, Merv walked me out to my car. In the course of polite conversation, I showed him the fender that needed repair.

"I'll fix that for you," he said.

Suddenly, I remembered my fleece for a husband. "Oh no!" I thought. "And this guy is a Christian, too!"

"How tall are you?" I blurted out.

"Six feet two and a half inches," he replied.

Hurray for the Red X's!

We were engaged the same day and married three months later. That was twelve years ago. Today, I'm divorced.

Where does the red X belong?

Somewhere I got the idea that being a Christian was like being on automatic pilot. Nothing can go wrong ... go wrong ... go wrong.... But it can and it does!

I used to fear those big red X's in my life, but I've come to realize that they are the times when I have grown the most. It's like a child learning to walk. At first, there are falls, but eventually the child will get it right and be able to walk, run, jump, skip, hop leap, and dance. I'm still falling down a lot, but I know that one day I'll be dancing. Hurray for the red X's!

There is no red X too big for the Lord to redeem. From every red X can come a blessing. The blessing is not always obvious at first. In fact, in the middle of some of my worst red X times, I've wondered whether God is paying attention. But I need to remember that God can bring good from all things—even from a red X.

If I had my life to live over, I'd make more mistakes next time. I would realize that I have to fall a few times before I learn to walk. I'd live in anticipation of the dancing to come, not in fear of the falls.

CHAPTER TWO

*"I'd relax.
I would limber up."*

Under
the
Mattress

When Nathan was placed in my arms at the age of three months, I had never held a baby, never changed a diaper, and never made a formula. I had been the only teenager in the neighborhood who had refused to baby-sit anything younger than two years old, and I had carried this dispassionate interest in babies into my adult years.

When we applied for adoption, the agency assured us that we wouldn't have a baby for at least six months—September at the earliest. My teaching job ended in June, so I had planned to spend most the summer visiting "baby owners"—sort of a practice run for this mother-to-be. But on the last day of school, my frantic husband called to say that our baby was on its way. I barely got home before the baby did.

From there on in, it was Nathan against the world. Never an easy child, he caught every rash that existed. With the price of oils and creams, we used to think that he had the most expensive piece of "bot-

Under the Mattress

tom land" in Canada. He was colicky, fretful, hyperactive, and anything but the warm, cuddly, little bundle that the baby cereal boxes had promised.

And I . . . well, I was the classic nervous mother. I felt so inadequate, so inexperienced. The advice poured in from every side, and it soon became abundantly clear to me that I was a failure at the mothering business. I just didn't seem to have the knack.

So I tried harder than ever and failed even more miserably. At the end of six weeks, I was finished. It seemed a nervous breakdown was just around the corner, and I was gratefully heading for the oblivion that such a breakdown would bring.

At this point, my mother arrived. Taking one look at her daughter and new grandson, she whisked us both home with her to Sudbury. I gratefully handed Nathan over to the experienced arms of "Granny," while I sank into a torpor of despair. I wasn't making it. What would happen to my son? Surely I would damage his psyche beyond repair with my inept fumblings at motherhood.

My mother's advice was invaluable: "Relax. Enjoy him. Don't take it all so seriously. If God gave you this baby, then God knows exactly the kind of mother you will be, and that kind of mother must be OK with God."

That was seven years ago.

Last week, I knew that I had finally gotten the idea.

The Daisies Are Still Free

Nathan and I were with some friends in a big local shopping mall. It was early evening, and the mall was crowded. We stopped at the eating area where a small band was playing. Their music was corny, prefifties, Big Band era, and the piano and saxophone were just no match for Guy Lombardo.

When they started playing "Stardust," I couldn't resist. Lifting Nathan up into my arms, I waltzed us around the tables full of munching families. Around and around we danced, cheek to cheek. Nathan loved it, and so did I. It had taken us seven years to learn to relax and enjoy each other.

At that moment, I felt I was more Nathan's mother than I ever had before, and I wasn't even working at it!

My relationship with my Lord is the same way. Somewhere inside, my prophet of doom tells me that I have to work at being a Christian. I feel that it isn't supposed to be easy, and certainly not relaxed. If my body and soul aren't bowed down under the weight of being a Christian, then I'm doing it all wrong.

I allow myself to be weighed down very easily. Once when my husband and I were serving a charge in Newfoundland, I had gotten very tired. As I am apt to do, I had taken on more things than I could handle. Physically, I was tired out. But even more important, I was tired out spiritually, too. I was so busy trying to be a superperson, that I had forgotten to relax and enjoy the Lord's company.

Under the Mattress

One weekend, Merv went away to a conference, and I had the manse all to myself. It was early Saturday morning when I got the bright idea to change the mattresses. We'd discussed changing our mattress for the better one in the small room next door, but like a lot of other things, we hadn't gotten around to it.

I decided to tackle the job myself. It was relatively easy, albeit a little clumsy. Move spring and mattress from one room and install on bedstead; place spring and mattress from other room onto other bedstead.

All went smoothly. I managed to move the double mattress from bedroom A to bedroom B without too much difficulty. After a great deal of heaving and shoving, I got the spring off the bedstead and slid it into the hall. I decided to leave it leaning against the wall of the narrow hallway while I then moved the mattress and spring from bedroom B to bedroom A, since bedroom B at this time was already overcrowded with the mattress from bedroom A. At this point, things were beginning to get a little complicated.

As I pushed the unwieldy mattress into the hall, it collapsed against the spring that was waiting to be moved. In a second, the spring slid over, pushing the mattress over also and pinning me against the wall. The spring continued to slide down until it wedged neatly from wall to wall with me and mattress fitted in underneath.

The Daisies Are Still Free

I couldn't crawl out the end since both bedroom doors opened side by side into the hall, and they were also wedged behind the spring. All the architects in the world could not have planned a bedspring, a mattress, and a hallway better designed to fit each other so neatly.

There I sat, completely helpless. There was no point in yelling, since the manse was located back from the road, and the mattress would muffle any sounds I might make. I could do nothing—nothing but sit under the mattress and think.

I sat for three hours in the hallway—quite comfortable, but trapped. You can get a lot of thinking done in three hours, and the Lord and I did a lot of business together behind the mattress and bedspring. When the work was done, and I had reestablished communication with my Savior, the back screen door opened and a voice called, "Anyone home?"

It was the chairman of the church board, and fortunately, he heard my muffled cries. In no time, I was rescued, the beds were rearranged, and George and I were enjoying a cup of tea. Another relationship was reestablished.

I am convinced that the heavens rang with angelic laughter that day as this too-busy-to-pray Christian sat underneath a mattress and prayed her heart out!

Under the mattress, I realized that my problem has always been that I forget to relax, to enjoy, to go with

Under the Mattress

the flow. I tend to get uptight, tense, worried. When that happens, the Spirit seems to shut down. I'm usually left in a worse state than before.

Somehow the Spirit needs a free channel through which to flow. When I clog up my pipes with tension and fear, the flow stops. The springs of living water dry up, and I'm barren and dry, too. It's only when I remember to limber up and relax that the Spirit flows freely, and I can enjoy the abundant life that there is for me.

If I had my life to live over, I'd remember the hours under the mattress. I'd remember to go with the flow.

CHAPTER THREE

*"I would be sillier
than I have been this trip.
I would take fewer
things seriously."*

The Singing Joy

Years ago, it was with the Armstrongs that I learned that the Christian walk is not only relaxed, but filled with joy as well. Ron is an Anglican priest. When I came to Toronto to board with his family, I was young, and you can well imagine my trepidation at the thought of holiness all the time. I was sure that was what I would find in a minister's household. Or so I thought.

The day I arrived at the rectory, Ron and June were in the midst of making candles. It was bazaar time at the church, and candles were their annual contribution to the Christmas tables.

The kitchen was an incredible sight—pots of melting wax on the stove, bits and pieces of Christmas tinsel and glitter strewn about, and candles. Candles being poured, candles cooling on the windows, candles being decanted from their molds, candles being decorated with whipped wax—candles everywhere.

In the midst of all this, I was aware that there was

The Singing Joy

something different about this family. It wasn't just that the time was right for fun. It was as if they were possessed of a well of joy within themselves. It was my first glimpse of what I came to call the "singing joy."

It didn't take long for me to feel at home. Holding a dripping pot of wax, I felt as if I had walked into a bright circle of fun.

I lived with the Armstrongs for nearly six months, and in all that time, my strongest memories are of laughter, fun, foolishness, and flights of fancy. Everything was an adventure—a ride in the car with the collapsible driver's seat, wallpapering the dining room ceiling at midnight, buying zany Christmas presents for everyone in the family.

There were moments of seriousness, too, and moments when the Spirit moved in power. There were moments of anger when tempers flared and tears when teenage temperaments clashed. But beneath it all, there was always a singing joy.

Several years ago, when I was in the midst of the break up of my marriage, I had forgotten this joy. I was so bound up within myself—holding my hurts inside, shutting out the world, pretending to be all right—that I completely lost touch with my inner light and my singing joy.

It was in this state that I reluctantly agreed to go to the Faith at Work Leadership Training Institute II. I really went just to get away from my situation, to take

The Daisies Are Still Free

some time to think through the relationship, and to try to salvage what I could of my crumbling life. I certainly didn't go to have fun.

But the Lord always knows what we need most. I didn't need the solitude that I had planned to find. I didn't need to do anymore inward looking or spiritual wrestling. I needed to get in touch with the singing joy.

And that's what happened.

Anyone who attended that week-long event will no doubt remember our group, if only for our noise. From the moment we met, we laughed. We celebrated life like children. We danced, sang, played games, joked, stayed up late, went for long walks, gorged ourselves on a doughnut binge, hugged a lot, and laughed a lot. Most of our tears were tears of joy, not of sorrow.

That week was one of the greatest gifts that my Lord has ever given me. It was a gift of laughter, light, and joy in the midst of the darkest time of my life. For a week, I put aside the nightmare around me and just enjoyed *being*.

It was a real discovery for me to find that the singing joy was still there just waiting to be released from within.

There are still so many times when I lose touch with the singing joy. I allow the pressures and frustrations of my world to squeeze it into a little, hard ball.

The Singing Joy

If I had my life to live over, I would allow the singing joy to completely fill me, surround me, encompass me, squeezing out those circumstances of my world which bind me.

CHAPTER FOUR

"I would take more chances."

Grab at a Chance

I once read a book about two middle-aged people who decided to sail their small boat around the world. The story of their adventure was exciting reading in itself, but the part that has always stayed in my memory was the words they had carved over the companionway of their yacht: "Grab at a chance and you'll never be sorry for a might-have-been."

In theory, I like to believe that I follow that maxim. It fits with the free spirit that I fondly imagine myself to be. Alas, in real life, it's a different story! There is always that little prophet of doom who delights in pointing out the cataclysmic things destined to happen if I grab at a chance. The prophet reminds me that my small risk will undoubtedly affect the cycle of the tides, the shape of the heavens above, or, at the very least, the grains of sand upon the earth. From there, it isn't hard to reach the point where I believe that the almighty "me" is the center of this universe, and God will have trouble keeping the stars on their course if I happen to risk a little.

Grab at a Chance

The only way I can grab at a chance is to beat my prophet to the punch. Unflinchingly, I ask myself, "What is the worst possible thing that can happen if I grab this chance?"

Of course, when I've identified the earthshaking consequences of my risk, their inconsequential degree of influence on the next ten thousand years of history becomes immediately obvious. Even I am able to admit that perhaps God, who owns the cattle on a thousand hills, can manage to deal with my consequences.

Occasionally the chance is so overwhelmingly tempting that neither I nor the small prophet have anything to say about the matter. Last summer, driving back from Toronto with friends, I was offered the opportunity to buy a small sailboat. Without thinking, I grabbed the chance. Sight unseen (such was my faith in the boat's owner), I said yes and closed the deal. Somewhere between Hamilton and Toronto, I became the owner of a small dinghy. I arranged to have it picked up in several weeks' time and rushed down to the cottage to make all the arrangements for my new toy.

I scoured the local library for all the books on sailing that I could find and read each one cover to cover, memorizing the launching procedure, how to make sail, and anything else I thought might come in handy.

The Daisies Are Still Free

It wasn't as though I had never sailed before. One summer, I had been a nervous crew for my experienced husband, learning the "art" in a twelve-foot dinghy. Although, to be perfectly honest, my experience consisted solely of hoisting and lowering the jib. I'm sure I must have held the tiller once or twice, but I truly don't remember doing so.

When we bought a twenty-six-foot "real" boat, I was even more nervous and found it best to busy myself below on every possible occasion when I might be called upon to do something nautical.

Of course, I had read every known book on cruising, enthusiastically joining in Merv's pipe dream of a trip around the world in our own boat. With him, I pored over endless boat plans, and, if nothing else, my theory and head knowledge couldn't be faulted.

However, I hadn't actually ever sailed a boat by myself. "Details, details," I chided myself. Why this little boat will be just a plastic bathtub toy. A six-year-old could sail it.

Then the sailboat arrived. From the moment we started loading the boat onto the truck, I realized that this was a little more than the toy I had expected. It wasn't a toy—it was a boat, and it was mine. Everyone was thrilled except the captain. In my heart of hearts, I doubted my ability to sail the darn thing. However, I managed to look nonchalant and confident.

The next day, I decided to rig the boat while it sat

Grab at a Chance

on the lawn—sort of a dry run. In broad daylight, it looked even larger and heavier than I had remembered from the night before. My mind told me it was only nine feet long, but my heart saw a twenty-foot yacht.

Fortunately, it was too heavy for me to carry to the river's edge, so I was able to stall for time while I had a special hand trailer made on which to trundle it along the road. In time, the trailer was ready, and I had no other excuse.

Before the prophet of doom could get a word in, I asked myself, "What's the worst thing that can happen?"

"I can drown." Unlikely. I was wearing a life jacket, and I was a good swimmer.

"The boat can sink." Not a chance. It had built-in flotation devices.

"I can make a fool of myself in front of my family and the entire Port Maitland Yacht Club."

That's the one that did it! It stopped me cold.

Make a fool of myself! I was just beginning to "get it together," to convince myself that I could handle things on my own. What was I doing putting myself in a position where I might not make it? Everyone knew that Merv had been the sailor in the family. What was I trying to prove anyway? Who was I trying to convince?

It was a long thirty yards from the cottage to the

launching ramp. I trudged along, pulling the boat behind me, surrounded by my excited children, my mother, the dog, and my friend Diane, who has always believed that I can do anything.

I glanced across the river to the yacht club. The docks were crowded, and several larger sailboats were already out on the river. No chance for an anonymous moment here.

We duly launched the dinghy in fine style, pouring the remains of an abandoned liquor bottle over her stubby bow, and wishing her fair winds.

I stepped aboard—or rather, I waded out in waist-deep water and rolled over the gunwale, scraping my shins in the process. Mentally, I ran through the lists I had memorized. I put all the right ropes in all the right places and hoisted up the sail. The wind caught the sail, and in moments, I was midriver.

I sailed the boat—or, I should say, *we* sailed it. The Man who stilled the waters sat beside me, and it was one of the best moments I've ever had. The main sheet was wrapped around my ankles, the sail sagged badly in one corner, and a miscellaneous rope or two trailed behind us in the water, but none of these things could quell the surge of self-confidence I felt as I brought the boat back to shore. I knew then that I—we—were going to make it!

I called the boat *Little Heart's Ease*, and it is. It is a

Grab at a Chance

might-have-been that I will never be sorry for.

When I look at things in light of their coming to me from God, I begin to see that some of what I have always thought of as chances are really "God incidences." Perhaps they are just possibilities put in front of me, and I have the option to take them or not to take them. My life may not be any smaller if I choose not to take one of these "God incidences"—grab at a chance—but, on the other hand, it may be all the richer if I do.

If I had my life to live over, I would grab at a chance, believing that it has come to me through God.

CHAPTER FIVE

*"I would take more trips.
I would climb more mountains
and swim more rivers."*

Pruning
the
Rosebushes

A few years ago, I faced serious surgery which jarred me out of my complacency. In the two weeks between my initial visit to the doctor and my admission to the hospital, I did some serious thinking about my life. One thing became very clear to me. I certainly wouldn't be able to leave this world believing that I had lived my life in the abundance that had been promised to me.

When I awoke in my hospital room and found that although a few bits and pieces were missing, I was still basically intact. I felt as if I had been given a second chance. As I convalesced, I took the time to work through some changes I planned to make in my life.

Without my being aware of it, my life had become increasingly ruled by a disease I call the "must-ought-shoulds." Everything I did was backed by the feeling that I "must" do it or "ought" to do it or "should" do it. Whether I actually wanted to do it—or more im-

Pruning the Rosebushes

portantly, whether the Lord wanted me to do it—was never really taken into consideration.

As a result, my life was cluttered up with many things that I didn't really enjoy. My time had become a whirlpool of meaningless activity. I was busy, but unfulfilled—active, but stagnant. I was doing all the "right" things, but I was unhappy doing them. When I looked over the past few years, I could see that the "must-ought-shoulds" had stolen my freedom just to *be*.

I had been given a second chance, and I was determined to claim that freedom back. It was a lot easier to say than do.

A month passed, and I was nowhere nearer that freedom than I had ever been. Somehow, I lacked the intestinal fortitude to make the changes that I knew my life needed. Slowly, I allowed myself to be wooed back into the life I had lived before my trip to the hospital. My hours were once again filled with useless meetings, endless discussions, and the changeless patterns that I had vowed to leave behind. Somewhere, something had gone wrong.

It was while I was pruning the rosebushes that I found the answer. I had planted the rosebushes at the cottage against the advice of every gardening expert. Everything was wrong for roses, they told me. The ground was pure sand—bone dry in summer and frozen in winter. The location was open to the cold

The Daisies Are Still Free

breezes and autumn gales from the lake. The area was too shady, the air was too damp, the weather was too cool, but I wanted roses at the cottage.

So, I bought half a dozen of the hardiest bushes I could find, and optimistically lacing them with bone meal, peat moss, and fertilizer, I planted them. They received more love and attention than my family that spring. They rewarded my care with new growth, and, against all odds, a bloom or two on each shoot!

The following spring, I again read every book on the subject of rose care and prepared to lavish the rosebushes with renewed attention in anticipation of an even greater abundance of blooms. Then I read about pruning. I was instructed to prune my babies—to sever their spindly limbs and mutilate their hardy branches—all for a vague promise of more and better roses.

Feeling like an executioner, I prepared to prune the roses. I studied the first bush carefully, mentally choosing the victims of my shears. I couldn't seem to begin. How could I cut out the vigorous new growth springing from the base of the bush? Surely in each shoot were multitudes of blossoms waiting to be born. How could I nip off the tender tips, knowing that from the same branch had come last year's best blooms? How could I be sure that the dead wood really had no life lurking in it, waiting for an opportunity to spring into bud and flower.

Pruning the Rosebushes

I hated pruning my roses. But I did, and only another gardener will understand when I say I asked their forgiveness. That summer, the roses grew and blossomed—tenfold, thirtyfold, a hundredfold!

And then it was spring again, and I realized that my life needed the same treatment. If pruning the rosebushes had set them free to bloom more abundantly, then pruning my life should set me free to be more abundant.

I started with the new shoots of "busyness" springing up in my life—things to which I had agreed because I was too undisciplined to say no, things which I thought I "must," "ought," or "should" do. I pruned them all out.

I called chairpersons and resigned, told leaders that I was unavailable, canceled courses, and opted out of committees. It was a heady experience! Whole blocks of time began to open up before me.

Then I looked at the "deadwood" in my life. These were the things that I had always done, either through habit or laziness. Now I examined each thing and judged it by two criteria: Did I really want to do it? Did Jesus really want me to do it?

Some things I wanted to do, but realized that they weren't places where the Lord wanted me to be. Other things I would have loved to leave behind, but the gentle voice of God reminded me that I had been put there for a purpose.

The Daisies Are Still Free

I left the choir, but remained in the prayer group. I gave up teaching at the Y, but continued with my evening classes.

All of this pruning proved painful to me and to those around me. People who had always counted on my inability to say no found it difficult to deal with this new creature who could not only say no, but didn't feel obliged to make excuses for her refusal. My husband, who had come to expect my support for all new groups and activities, didn't really understand why I wouldn't attend just because I "ought" to. I found it hard to force myself to prune. After all, life may have been unsatisfactory in my hectic rut, but at least it didn't make any waves.

By the time fall rolled around, I had claimed back my freedom to *be*. I could climb any mountain I thought needed climbing, swim any river that looked inviting, or take a side trip if it beckoned to me. Only two criteria were required to make my decision: Did I want to do it? Did Jesus want me to do it?

One Sunday, I was asked to take the morning service at church. I decided to share my pruning with the congregation. The message was clear, and it was exciting to watch as people began to free up their lives. The dull pattern of the church fabric began to glow with new, vibrant colors as those who had felt they "should" be in the kitchen joined the choir, those who thought they "must" teach Sunday school

Pruning the Rosebushes

came to the pews to worship, and those who believed they "ought" to serve on the church board became a part of the fellowship group. The resulting tapestry—as it had been with my own life, and as it had been with the roses—was infinitely more beautiful than before.

If I had my life to live over, I would remember to prune my life—to claim the freedom to climb my mountain, swim my river, or take my trip!

CHAPTER SIX

*"I would eat more ice cream
and less beans."*

Chocolate Sundae Heaven

It was one of those hot steamy days in Toronto when everyone is anxious to get to work, if for no other reason than the pleasure of leaving the crammed subway car for a cool air-conditioned office. I was no exception.

As I gratefully sank into my chair and let the cooling breeze of the air vents blow across my face, I decided that I would not venture out again until I had to leave at five o'clock. I could enjoy lunch in the small office cafeteria, and never leave the sixty-eight degrees of comfort.

It was a busy morning in our office. A lot of things were going on, and the lunch hour passed by without anyone noticing. It was nearly two o'clock before any of us thought about eating.

We decided to go to the small lunchroom on the third floor. When we got there, we discovered that everyone else in the building had made the same decision. Ten floors of hungry workers had completely wiped out the supplies of the small kitchen. A few

Chocolate Sundae Heaven

packages of cookies and little else remained on the bare counters.

No one suggested that we should seek food elsewhere. The baking heat shimmered against the windows. We decided to send out one brave soul to bring back a lunch for all of us.

The area around the office abounds with many small restaurants, catering to every kind of taste—Mexican, Italian, Greek, Chinese, a delicatessen. The problem was not how to get our lunch, but where to get it. We couldn't agree on which cuisine to choose.

In the midst of our good-natured wrangling, when it became obvious that our pocketbooks and palates were never going to find common ground, someone made a suggestion.

"If everyone will give me $1.50, I'll go out and buy lunch."

"$1.50! Where can you find lunch for that price?"

She smiled. "Lunch will be a surprise. If you're willing to take a chance, I'll go and get you my favorite lunch."

We looked at her dubiously. She seemed healthy, normal. Her favorite lunch couldn't be all that much of a risk. And none of us wanted to consider the alternative of the tropical heat outside. Any kind of food, as long as someone else fetched it, seemed a good idea.

It was with a real spirit of adventure that we each counted out our $1.50.

The Daisies Are Still Free

"I'll be back in fifteen minutes," she said.

Fifteen minutes! That wasn't much time for any kind of fancy preparation. We decided that she must have the local deli in mind, but, as someone pointed out, you can't get much there for $1.50.

In less than fifteen minutes, she was back, carrying a large white paper bag. It didn't look very big, considering how many lunches were supposed to be in it.

We crowded around her desk as she opened the bag. Inside were several smaller bags, all tightly closed. No smells wafted out. "Not Chinese," murmered a disappointed voice.

She handed a small bag to each of us, warning us to keep them right side up. The bags felt cold.

And inside ... a chocolate sundae. Three scoops of ice cream—chocolate mocha, French vanilla, and chocolate mint—smothered in "hot" fudge sauce and topped off with whipped cream and walnuts.

There was a moment of stunned silence. Then began the protests.

"Ice cream! For lunch?"

"Oh, no. There goes my diet!"

"Think of all the calories!"

"I never eat chocolate. It's bad for my complexion."

"But I'm hungry for some real food."

And so on. But our messenger remained unmoved. She continued to smile at us and made no effort to justify her choice.

Chocolate Sundae Heaven

Resignedly, we began to nibble the ice cream. And something happened. Slowly, with mounting enthusiasm, people began eating their sundaes. The room grew quiet, broken only by sighs of delight. We grinned at one another over the tops of our ice cream cups, crunching the walnuts with noisy relish and licking our spoons.

Memories of other sundaes in kinder times and younger years surrounded us. Some closed their eyes, savoring the tastes that were usually unknown in our egg-salad-sandwich-and-nourishing-soup world.

Gone was the heat of the outside and the thoughts of the five o'clock rush. Gone was the frustration of impending deadlines, broken typewriters, paychecks and deductions, mortgages, or car troubles.

We were in chocolate sundae heaven! For fifteen brief minutes, we were living in the now, enjoying the taste of chocolate ice cream and fudge sauce.

Living for today, in the now, is a lot easier said than done. I once leased my apartment for the summer while I went away to work at a girls' camp. I came back in September to find that my tenants had left the rent unpaid, the cupboards bare, and the utilities turned off.

I had only the money that I had earned from my summer job. I was due to start teaching the following Monday, although the paycheck wouldn't arrive until the end of the month.

The Daisies Are Still Free

I was honest enough to realize that it was important to pay the rent and the utility bills. By the time my rent was up to date, my phone, lights, and heat back on, and my car filled with gas, I had fifty-seven cents, a can of mushroom soup, and six tea bags to last me until the end of the month.

But, I didn't panic. Why not? Because I had a credit card. I knew that this card could buy me food, clothing, gas, entertainment—anything that I might need. The fact that I had no money to back the credit card didn't bother me at all. I'd pay it all off . . . next month.

That was Friday. I couldn't sleep Friday night. I tossed and turned, and through my mind ran the words "Do not be anxious about your life, what you shall eat, nor about your body, what you shall put on" (Luke 12:22).

I knew what it was all about. I had done a lot of preaching to other people about relying on the Lord for everything, about stepping out in faith, and about trusting God to supply my needs. When it came right down to the crunch, the only thing I was trusting in or relying on or stepping out with was my credit card! No wonder I had insomnia.

There was only one thing to do. In a moment of supreme confidence (or madness, depending upon your point of view), I leaped out of bed and cut my credit card into shreds with a pair of scissors. Just to make

Chocolate Sundae Heaven

sure that I wouldn't be tempted to glue it back together, I flushed the pieces down the toilet!

I wish I could say that at that moment I felt uplifted, conscious of God's hand on me, or even a small surge of faith, but I didn't. The only thing I felt was absolute panic. Now I had done it. I had fifty-seven cents and little else until the end of the month. Even if I reapplied for the card, it would be at least a week or two before it was processed.

I didn't sleep well at all that night.

On Saturday I ate the can of mushroom soup and used up two of the tea bags.

By Saturday night my three-square-meals-a-day stomach was complaining about the treatment. But I was helpless. There was nothing I could do.

"Well, Lord," I thought. "It's up to you now. I'll put my faith where my mouth is, literally!"

Late Saturday night the phone rang. It was friends inviting me to lunch after church the next day. Well, one meal taken care of. Thank you, Lord.

Sunday breakfast was tea, black. Then, lunch with the Warrens. There I met the man I was to marry, and he took me for supper at his friends' house. Two meals, Lord. They gave me a "doggy bag" to take home. Lunch for Monday, Lord. And on Monday, the same man, to whom I was now engaged, arrived at my apartment after work.

Was he bringing me roses, candy, or a ring? No, he

The Daisies Are Still Free

was carrying a big bag of groceries, and even he has never been able to explain why he bought them for me.

On Tuesday, without precedent, the North York School Board paid an advance on the September salary. The rest is history.

I still forget that eating the ice cream means that I don't worry about the beans for the pot. I'm always asking the Lord to take care of me, but I don't expect the Lord to do it.

If I had my life to live over, I would eat more ice cream and less beans. I'd truly realize that when I am being what I was created to be, this is a chocolate sundae world for me. Lilies were created to be lilies; I was created to be me. And when I am being me, I need only sit at the feet of Jesus and adore him—enjoy the ice cream. After all, the beans are his department.

CHAPTER SEVEN

"I would perhaps have more actual troubles, but I'd have fewer imaginary ones."

There's No Such Thing as a Dragon

I once read a wonderful children's book called *There's No Such Thing as a Dragon* by Jack Kent. In the story, a little boy wakes up one morning to find a tiny dragon in his room. The dragon follows the boy down to breakfast and cheerfully devours all the pancakes on the table. When the little boy complains to his mother, she says, "Don't be silly. There's no such thing as a dragon."

Throughout the day, the mother keeps bumping into the dragon, and each time she does, she says, "There's no such thing as a dragon." Each time she denies it exists, the dragon grows a little larger. Eventually it grows so large that it fills the whole house. In one delightful scene, it and the house walk away.

Fortunately, the postman had noticed the house and dragon walk by, and he is able to tell the family where to find them. Mother finally admits that the dragon does exist after all. As she does, the dragon shrinks back to its original tiny self. "He just wanted to be recognized," explains the little boy.

There's No Such Thing as a Dragon

I have a similar imaginary dragon in my life. It's called "What If," and it lurks in the corners of my mind, waiting for me to admit that it's there. Of course, I don't care to acknowledge any doubts I may have about my life, so I steadfastly ignore "What If" and blindly hope that it will go away.

From that point on, "What If" becomes the unspoken thought—the imaginary dragon—behind everything I do. Sometimes I am able to deny its existence so successfully that it grows to an incredible size and completely paralyzes my life.

Recently, I felt that I should leave St. Catharines and move to Toronto. That meant leaving a job, finding a job, selling a house, finding a house, and moving with two kids, two cats, a mother, and a dog!

Whenever I get a feeling that I suspect is a message from the Lord, I chew it over, worry it like an old dog with a bone. Then I try to decide just how far my faith is going to carry me.

The idea of moving to Toronto barely got off the ground. Old "What If" was lurking in some dark corner, just waiting for an opportunity to blow cold water (as opposed to the usual fire-breathing variety) over the whole thing.

Leave my job! "What if they hear that you're looking around, and they jump the gun and fire you?" "What if you can't find a job as good as the one you already have?" "What if you leap from the frying pan

The Daisies Are Still Free

into the fire? At least you know where you are now."

Find a new job! "What if no one wants to hire you? You're not getting any younger, you know." "What if you get into a crummy situation, and you're stuck in it?" "What if you get laid off or fired because you have no seniority or tenure?"

Sell my house! "What if it doesn't sell? You know what the market is like these days." "What if you can't get enough from the sale to clear your equity?"

Buy another house! "What if you can't find a house that is big enough for all of the family?" "What if you can't afford a house in Toronto?" "What if no one will give you a mortgage?" "What if you have to rent? Who'll rent to your menagerie?"

Move the family! "What if you can't afford a moving company?" "What if no one will help you?" "What if it rains on moving day?"

You can see how it wasn't hard for old "What If" to squelch the idea of moving to Toronto.

Of course, I didn't admit that "What If" had anything to do with my decision to stay put. I just decided that the idea wasn't really a message from the Lord, and I was much better off where I was already.

But, if you've ever been led by the Lord, you know how hard it is to ignore. That's how it was with the idea of moving. At every opportunity, it surfaced in my mind. Each time, I'd pause just long enough for "What If" to get in its two cents' worth, and then I'd

There's No Such Thing as a Dragon

put the idea away, telling myself that I was just being silly. Why on earth would the Lord want me to move?

At the end of November, the idea surfaced once more. I was teaching in a private school and needed to give at least a month's notice. If I gave notice then, I could leave at Christmas, use the Christmas vacation to pack, and move in at the beginning of the New Year. The children could start their new school with the rest of the children returning from holidays, and everything would fall neatly into place.

It sounded great—theoretically.

I spent a week trying to make the decision. I felt so strongly that this was the Lord's will for me . . . and yet . . . what if?

"The Lord can't possibly want me to step out this way since I need to have everything settled before I give my notice."

"What If" had won another round!

Two weeks before Christmas, I saw a job advertised in the Toronto paper that looked promising. I applied for it. I was hired at my interview a week later.

Three days after my house went on the market, it sold on an unconditional offer for the price I needed. Two days after that, I found a house in Toronto— exactly what we all wanted, and at a price that even I could afford. Some friends offered to help me move by renting the moving van and driving it to Toronto.

The Daisies Are Still Free

Everything was perfect, except for one "minor" detail. I couldn't give my notice at work until we returned from Christmas holidays. That meant I couldn't leave until the first week in February. Everything had to be put off until that point.

The ramifications were far-reaching: I had to commute to Toronto for three weeks. We moved at the end of Februrary, on the coldest day of the year, but we weren't able to get into our new house ahead of moving day to do some badly needed cleaning and minor repairs.

Oh, "What If," you really messed that one up! You grew so large that I ran away rather than face you down.

If I had my life to live over, I would admit that there is a "What If" dragon in my life. I would face it, recognizing its disguise as my worst doubts and fears and anxieties. I would be free to see it for what it really is—a small, dark corner of my heart where I allow no one in, not even Jesus.

Having admitted that it is there, I would be able to see the light of Jesus shine on it, shrivel it to infinity, and banish it from my life. I would perhaps have more actual troubles, but I'd have fewer imaginary ones.

CHAPTER EIGHT

*"You see, I'm one of those
people who live sensibly and
sanely hour after hour,
day after day."*

The
Great, Gray
Bird

Sometimes, I think that I must have a split personality.

There is the sane, logical, sensible side of me—the side that always looks at things calmly and rationally, advocating a sensible solution to a thorny problem. This is the side which hands out good, down-to-earth advice to those less fortunate people who let their emotions rule their lives.

I'm comfortable with this side of my personality. At least I know exactly where I am. The waters are never disturbed, no one rocks any emotional boats, and life can be counted on to go steadily—albeit dully—to a logical conclusion.

I've always tried to cultivate my sensible side. After all, my life could use a lot more sense and order than it has. If any emergency arises, I first consult my sensible self, hoping my sensible self will find a way to keep me uninvolved. After all, I certainly don't need that kind of upset. I've got problems of my own.

The Great, Gray Bird

My sensible self usually manages very well, and I can relax and know that I dealt with the problem in a sane manner. "In an adult manner," whispers my little prophet.

As much as possible, I try to keep the other side of my personality under wraps. For one thing, my alter ego can be terribly embarrassing, laughing at the wrong time, crying at the wrong moment, doing irrational things during emergencies, and never, never doing what is sensible. My other self seems to be tuned into the stream of the Spirit that bypasses our earthly strivings and flows directly to the heart of God.

Though wonderful in a spiritual situation—when it's all right to be a little emotional or to be a little more intuitive than normal—in everyday life I find it best to ignore my emotional half as much as possible. If I'm not careful, I could be labeled a "kook."

I will admit, though, that sometimes there are moments that would be lost if my sensible self were allowed full control—moments when I come close to the throne of God and catch a glimpse of the Kingdom. I remember one such time well. Perhaps it stays with me because it answered a need within me. Perhaps it was a moment when God's grace will forever remain crystal clear to me.

The cold, gray days of autumn were slowly coming to a close, and I had driven down to the cottage to

The Daisies Are Still Free

help my mother pack up for the season. Cottage closing is always a sad time at best. So many memories are put away with the beach towels and lawn chairs. Another summer come and gone. Golden days lost, never to return.

That closing day seemed worse than any before. The weather was cold, with a steady rain driving from the east. The leaves had long since left the trees, and the ground was covered with a sodden blanket. All the other cottages were already closed and boarded up. Their shuttered fronts gleamed slickly under the onslaught of the rain. Sulky gray skies hung low over the river, and even a fire couldn't dispel the air of damp in the cottage.

As soon as I arrived, mother pointed out the great, gray bird to me. In a small clearing between our cottage and the one next door, it stood close against the wall under the dripping branches of an alder tree. The gray bird was one of the beautiful, blue herons that we often watched fly overhead, but I had never seen one this close before.

Obviously there was something wrong with the bird. It made no attempt to fly away, but slowly turned in circles, its plumage dripping with rain. Its eyes were hooded, and it seemed unaware that we were so close.

Immediately, the sensible me wanted to do something about the poor creature. I called every wildlife

The Great, Gray Bird

service and protection agency within a hundred miles. No one was interested in a soggy heron at a cottage ten miles from the nearest town. It was late Friday afternoon, and most workers had left the office. When anyone answered, the lack of interest was dismaying. "Call back on Monday," advised one government agency.

There was nothing I could do. I put on my jacket and walked over to see if I could frighten the heron into flying away. It ignored my footsteps, and only the sheer size of the great, gray bird made me keep my distance.

I returned to the cottage, determined to forget it. After all, there was nothing, absolutely nothing, I could do to help.

As I went about the ritual of cottage-closing tasks, I found myself continually drawn to the window and to the great, gray bird beneath the alder tree. Soon, everything was packed, and it was time to lock up and leave.

But something within me just would not let me drive away and leave the bird, which was endlessly circling the tree in the rain. It was so much like the feelings that were within me—the parts of my life that were hidden behind the beating rain. I felt that I, too, had been circling for a long time. For a moment, the bird was all that I sensed. I had to do something for it. Once again, I put on my jacket, and leaving the fam-

The Daisies Are Still Free

ily to their last cup of tea, I walked over to the bird.

The rain beat down heavier than before with a touch of ice in its breath. I was soon chilled, and I wondered how long the bird had been there.

Approaching it slowly, I came as close as I dared. I squatted down and as I did so, it opened its eyes and looked directly at me. We stared at each other for several moments. The circling ceased.

Then, that side of me which listens to the voice of the Spirit took over. I started to pray for the great, gray bird. I prayed for its hurts and its healing. I told the bird of the love of Jesus and my love. I told it how beautiful it was when it flew overhead and that it was free to fly again, to begin its long journey to the warm southland. I prayed until I had no words left. In all that time, it didn't move.

Slowly I walked away, a little ashamed at the tears that wet my cheeks. Putting the last few things in the car, I looked back. It still hadn't moved.

I returned to the cottage to dampen down the fire. As I drew the curtains shut, the sky suddenly cleared over the river, and a thin beam of sunshine crept between the black clouds. And then I saw the great, gray bird—free, beautiful, strong—winging up and over the river and turning to the south in a deep, banking glide.

And I was free, too!

The Great, Gray Bird

If I had my life to live over, I would allow the side of me that moves in the Spirit to move into my life fully and set me free to *be*.

CHAPTER NINE

*"Oh, I've had my moments,
and if I had it to do over
again, I'd have more of them.
In fact, I'd try to have nothing else.
Just moments, one after another,
instead of living so many years
ahead of each day."*

Living in the Now

Have you ever experienced a moment in time that remains with you for the rest of your life? Sometimes a word, a turn of phrase, or a familiar melody will bring it all flooding back.

That's how it is with me every time I hear "The Old Rugged Cross." As the first notes strike my ear, a special moment is relived in my mind.

I belonged to a large interdenominational choir. We were all ordinary people from different faiths and different backgrounds who gathered together because we loved to sing and we loved the same Lord.

One evening, we were halfway through our regular practice in a local church, when a shabby, unkempt fellow stumbled into the sanctuary. He reeked of alcohol, and I found myself shrinking back as he shambled down the aisle past my seat.

Finding a nearby pew, he seemed to settle into a drunken slumber. Several songs later, Henry, our director, called for a break. The drunk seemed to rouse and, looking about, said to Henry, "I used to sing,

Living in the Now

too, you know. I wasn't always like this." His words were slurred, but tears stood out distinctly in his eyes.

"What did you sing, friend?" asked Henry.

The man paused for a moment, a faraway look in the bleary eyes. "I remember 'The Old Rugged Cross.'"

Henry took the man's arms and led him over to the piano. "Play for my friend," he instructed the pianist.

As she struck the opening chord, Henry turned the man to face him and, placing his hands on the dirty shoulders, looked directly into the filthy, unshaven face. With love and deep compassion, Henry sang the old, old story. Slowly, the members of the choir joined in, blending their voices in unwritten harmonies.

It was a golden moment as the truth of that old gospel hymn reached out and touched the heart within that broken body. When the song finished, the man brushed his hand across his eyes. Henry hugged him, and we joined in prayer for this man. Slowly the derelict turned and left the church.

I do not know if that one lonely life was saved that night, but I do know that my life was irrevocably changed by what happened.

Everytime I hear "The Old Rugged Cross," I remember that Jesus died, not only for the good, the churchgoer, and the holy, but also for the tramp, the

The Daisies Are Still Free

drunk, and the derelict. Most of all, I remember that Jesus died for me.

There are so few moments in my life when I see beyond the external, and I am touched by the hand of the Lord. I want those moments to happen as and how I expect them to happen. That night in the choir, I nearly lost a precious moment because I only saw the social implications of a drunk in God's house.

I need to learn to be like a little child who never looks beyond the moment, but takes all that it has to offer. The child stops by the wayside to pick up a stone to feel its contours and to test its weight. The feel of that particular rock will stay with that child for a long time.

Sometimes, I get a brief glimpse of what a life of moments would be like. A walk on the beach is made up of moments—the sound of the waves, the wind at my back, the feel of the sand under my feet. The sight of a tiny shell nestled in a drift of debris. The smell of hot rocks in the sun. The cry of sea gulls overhead.

These are moments that I find easy to keep. Is it because they are more tangible than the spiritual moments that often elude me? Or is it because I allow my whole being to become part of the beach, the sun, and the wind?

When I sang "The Old Rugged Cross" along with Henry, I allowed myself to become one with the music, the words, and the moment.

Living in the Now

If I had my life to live over, I would remember to savor moments as a child does, to become one with each and every one of them, and to live in the now of this moment—not in the possibility of the next.

CHAPTER TEN

"I've been one of those persons who never goes anywhere without a thermometer, a hot water bottle, a raincoat, and a parachute. If I had it to do again, I would travel lighter than I have."

"Ladybird, Ladybird, Fly Away Home"

I've always prided myself on the fact that things don't mean a lot to me. In the first five years of our marriage, we moved seven times. You do a lot of weeding out when you have to pack something seven times. By the fifth time around, you have a pretty good idea whether it's really something that you want to take with you again.

I've sold and given away furnishings for whole households without even batting an eye. The couch that I joyfully found in a garage sale and spent the rainy weekend recovering went out the door without a qualm. The pile of knickknacks I collected were ruthlessly thrown out somewhere between move four and move six.

Of course there are some things that have survived all the upheavals. I don't pretend that they aren't precious to me, but I also know that they would suffer the same fate as the rest of my "treasures," if it were necessary.

That makes me a real party pooper when it comes to

"Ladybird, Ladybird, Fly Away Home"

playing "house on fire." This is a well-known group game, the object of which is to center in on what is really important to you and why. The premise is that your house is on fire, and you can save any ten objects, assuming that all living things have been rescued. From there, you narrow it down to three objects. Hopefully you are then able to share what these three objects are and what meaning they have in your life. It's a surefire (pardon the pun) group starter.

The problem is that my list is so variable. I can never decide what I really want to save. Usually I end up claiming that I'd just as soon leave it all and start over again tomorrow.

If pressed, I will agree to rescue at least three things. A beautiful hand-turned egg—a wooden egg within an egg within an egg. It was a gift from my uncle, and he had it when he was a child. I keep it because it's a family thing—a link to the past that I didn't buy at an auction sale or find in a rummage bin.

An engraved silver bracelet. My mother gave it to me on my twenty-first birthday. She received one on her twenty-first birthday—a family tradition.

A small, framed needlepoint picture. It was my Christmas card from Marg. She embroidered it just for me, and it's special because I know that Marg has little time with five children to do these things.

I know, however, if it came right down to it, I'd leave even these things behind if I had to. They're

The Daisies Are Still Free

precious to me, but I can truly say that they are just things.

Perhaps that's why I shop for most of my household goods and clothes at Goodwill stores, economic considerations aside. I'm probably shopping for the past that I leave behind me each time I move. I love to sit in an old armchair I bought from the Salvation Army Store and speculate who else has enjoyed its comfort or find a hand-hooked rug and wonder what mind conceived the design, what eyes chose the colors, and whose fingers wove the patterns.

A well-worn quilt links me to a past and a world much kinder than the one I live in. I become part of a never-ending cycle—almost immortal—as things I had move on to new lives with someone else, and things I now have bind me to other lives I can only guess at.

Yes, I like to think that I travel light.

Recently, though, I have begun to realize that I'm fooling myself. I don't really travel light at all. Oh yes, I easily leave behind all the tangible things in my life, but subconsciously, I am rescuing a great suitcase full of intangibles from the fire which threatens my house.

I keep this suitcase by my side at all times. I never leave it behind. I'd feel helpless, defenseless without it.

What is in my suitcase? A change of socks or a toothbrush? No, nothing so mundane. A Bible or a scriptural promise? No nothing so spiritual either.

"Ladybird, Ladybird, Fly Away Home"

I carry protection in my suitcase—special items that will protect me from any situation that threatens my little inner core.

Most of the room in the suitcase is taken up by my very own wall. The wall is high—too high to climb over. It is made of heavy stone—too thick to knock down. There are no gates or doors in my wall, and it does what I designed it to do. It keeps people out.

Inside my wall I keep the real me—the vulnerable me, beset by fears, worries, anxieties. I don't want anyone inside the wall with me. They might laugh or feel pity or ridicule me.

Very few people have ever seen my wall; most don't even suspect that it is there. It is cleverly disguised with words such as: "I'm OK." "I'm strong." "I never doubt." "My life is great." "Everything is just great."

You can be sure that I always pack my wall in the suitcase. I also carry a great pile of freshly ironed dictums in my suitcase. Without these dictums, I'd never know if I was measuring up or not.

For instance, I have a whole set of dictums which tell me when I'm a good mother. There is one to tell me that a good mother always serves a nourishing breakfast to her family. The fact that neither mother nor family can face a fried egg at 8 A.M., that breakfast becomes a tangle of bad tempers and power plays has no bearing on the validity of this rule. Dictums are infallible.

The Daisies Are Still Free

I know if I'm a good housekeeper by the state of my bathroom. A good housekeeper always has the taps polished and matching towels on the racks, and there is never, never a ring around the bathtub or kids' dirty socks lying beside the hamper. Of course, if I'm a good housekeeper, there is a dictum that tells me I'm automatically a good wife and mother, too.

The dictums I've packed to govern my life as a Christian are just dandy. They are there for me to fall back on whenever I have any doubts or fears. There's an order to tell me that I should be full of the joy of the Lord at all times. I should also read my Bible daily, pray at least an hour in solitude, be a paragon of virtue at all times, and maintain a Christian attitude toward my neighbors. Now, that's a nice, solid dictum to live up to.

To govern the rest of my life, I have a rule for every situation:

"If it tastes good, it can't be good for you."

"Only babies cry."

"Better safe than sorry."

"Never get your hopes up."

"You can't trust anyone."

"Put on a happy face."

I've never met a dictum that I couldn't use. They are all neatly packed in my suitcase, ready for any emergency. Burn down, house. I'm OK!

The last item in my suitcase is a length of stout

"Ladybird, Ladybird, Fly Away Home"

rope. I keep it coiled and ready, just in case I'm ever required to make any leaps in faith. The rope is firmly attached to the "solid" things in my life—an insurance policy, a good job, friends who think I'm just great, money in the bank—things that I can lean on when this faith business gets a little rough.

With my suitcase by my side, I'm prepared for anything that life has to offer. My house can burn down around me, but I'm safe!

If I had my life to live over, I'd like to travel lighter than I have. I'd like to have my hands free to drop that suitcase, so that I can put my hand in the hand of God; and put out my hands to receive all that the Lord has to offer!

CHAPTER ELEVEN

*"If I had my life to live
over, I would start barefoot
earlier in the spring and
stay that way later in the fall."*

An
Exercise in
Sole Touching

I've always been fascinated by Henry VIII, and so when I had an opportunity to visit his palace, Hampton Court, I was eager to go. I was thrilled to see all the places I had only read about: the minstrel's gallery with its carved screens, the tennis courts, the giant vine, the maze, and the garden.

Everywhere I looked there was opulence and wealth—halls and galleries filled with priceless furniture and antique treasures and stone walls hung with beautiful tapestries and paintings. The grandeur of history permeated the vaulted ceilings and echoing passages.

Near the end of the day, I left the guided tour and slipped away to see the rest of the building alone.

Following a sloping, stone passageway, I stepped through a huge wooden door from the garden and found myself in the kitchen. Its sheer size and bulk were overwhelming. One side was made up of brick ovens—deep caverns built into the wall. How many countless loaves of bread and fine cakes had been

An Exercise in Sole Touching

baked in these ovens? How many pastries and treats, created to titillate the jaded palates of the court's lords and ladies?

At the other end of the room, the open hearth fireplace stood about six feet high, and nearly as wide. Huge iron spikes for holding the boiling caldrons were driven into the stonework, now blackened and charred with age. Over the room hung a miasma of dampness and disuse. No sunlight reached here; no stray summer breeze blew across the floors. It was cold and lifeless—a room with no purpose, dead and decaying.

I suddenly wanted to escape from this subterranean room, far below the beauties of the palace above. I hurried to the nearest doorway, intent on leaving the damp air and echoing spaces behind.

As I stepped over the stone threshold of the door, my foot caught on an irregularity in the stone slab. Looking down, I saw the perfect outline of a human foot about two inches deep, clearly delineated against the smooth surface of the stone around it.

How did it get there? Why had the builder put a footprint on the threshold?

Then I realized what had happened. For centuries, the cooks, scullions, servants, and underlings, who had peopled these giant caverns, had used this doorway to leave the kitchen. It was the only doorway that led to the rest of the palace, and whether it was the

The Daisies Are Still Free

cook's boy or the lord's serving man or the king himself, each would have to use this door.

Over the years, as people like me stepped up to the threshold, their feet met the same place on the stone. Like water dripping on a rock bed, the stone had slowly been worn away until a perfect footprint was left behind.

Impulsively, I kicked off my sandal and placed my foot into the print on the threshold. Suddenly, I was a part of all the history that had been in that place. I was one with those who had come before me, and I would become one with those who came after. By the simple touching of flesh on cold stone, I had become a part of that place—a drop in the sands of time that surrounded it.

Would I have felt the same if I had left my sandal on? I don't think so. It was the touch of the cold stone against my bare flesh that made the moment real. No artificial barrier existed between me and the place where so many other feet, both bare and shod, had gone before.

The experience lingered at the back of my mind for many years, but it wasn't until we were sent to Newfoundland that the truth of that moment was made clear to me.

On our last evening in Ontario, we had a home Communion service with our friends Kris and John

An Exercise in Sole Touching

Wood. It was our way of saying good-bye to each other, and it was our way of pledging our prayers and mutual support of each other, too.

Voicing my greatest fears, I silently asked the Lord to give me an assurance that we would not be completely alone in Newfoundland and that, although we would be apart from friends and family, we would still be a part of the fellowship.

The Communion service was beautiful. The four of us knelt in the living room, which was lighted only by the candles and surrounded by the sounds of the evening countryside—the cooing of the wood doves, the rustle of the leaves outside the open window.

At one point in the Communion these words were spoken: "Therefore with angels and archangels and the whole company of heaven, evermore praising thee and saying, 'Holy, holy, holy, Lord God Almighty. Hosanna in the highest. Blessed is he that cometh in the name of the Lord.' " As I listened to these words, I had a vision.

It seemed as if the walls of the room melted and dissolved in front of me. In their place, stretching up into the evening sky and blacking out the trees and fields beyond the room, I saw a phalanx of people, row upon row upon row. They were closely packed together, and the colors of their clothes glowed like jewels—the deep red of a bishop, the gold of a king, or the black garb of a pilgrim. Their faces were indis-

The Daisies Are Still Free

tinct, but I was aware of the costumes of different times, nationalities, and cultures.

Beyond this throng, there were further rows of shining, white beings—the angels and the host of heaven. Beyond the angels, a beautiful, white light, stretching and glowing across space and time. As we began the litany in the farmhouse room, I saw this great multitude assume the attitude of prayer, their clothes moving and shifting, and the wings of the angels rustling, as they bowed their heads. When we four said together, "Holy, holy, holy . . . ," the whole company of heaven joined with us.

It was the same moment that I had felt at Hampton Court. I was one with this great host, and they were one with me in the Spirit. My bare soul had reached out and joined with them. I would never again be lonely in my Christian walk.

If I had my life to live over, I would walk barefoot, allowing my spirit to become one with the Spirit who created me.

CHAPTER TWELVE

"I would go to more dances."

Dance to My Own Song

My daughter Cherith has always wanted to dance. From the time she could toddle, she has dreamed of being a "bally" dancer. When she discovered that there was such a thing as dancing lessons, she begged and pleaded with me to take her.

At four years of age, Cherith was long and slim, all bony elbows and knees, with straight, fine hair. She was forever bumping into things, as if she hadn't come to terms with her long arms and legs.

I decided that dancing lessons were perhaps just what she needed. Perhaps the lessons would help her to control her muscles and give her the grace to offset her height.

Cherith was ecstatic as we shopped for the pink tights, leotard, and soft dancing slippers, but the first time she dressed for her dancing class, I sensed that we were going to have some problems. The leotard hung around her body, since she had to have several sizes larger in order to fit her up and down. Her tights became known as "loosies" in our house because they

Dance to My Own Song

were loose. And the neat hair that was required by the school meant spray net, bobby pins, elastic bands, and tears.

But she loved the class from the moment she started. She was very reluctant, however, to show me what she was learning. So I was more than eager for parents' day. It was, they promised us, a preview of the dancing recital that would be held in the spring.

The mothers were told to wait in the dressing room while the little dancers got ready for us. Since I always went shopping during Cherith's class time, I hadn't made friends with any of the other mothers. Most of them seemed to be old hands at the business, talking about the various recitals and performances their children had been in. I was relieved when we were finally ushered into the studio.

About sixteen little girls were standing along the bar in front of a huge, wall mirror. Cherith stood out from the rest for two reasons. She was by far the tallest child in the row, and she was utterly captivated by her reflection in the mirror. It was obvious that she thought she was beautiful.

I looked at her in dismay. The neat hairdo was down around her ears with stray wisps hanging over her eyes. Her panties showed below the leotard. Her "loosies" hung in folds around her ankles, and one bow on the shiny pink slippers had come undone.

I heard a muttered comment and a giggle from

The Daisies Are Still Free

somewhere down the row of mothers. I decided to assume that they weren't talking about my daughter.

The music started, and the dancers dutifully lined up, except Cherith, who was still gazing at herself in the mirror. Gently, one of the instructors placed her in line with the others.

With practiced ease, the children performed their little dance. "I'm a little teapot, short and stout...." Handles and spouts were duly presented, tipped over, and poured out—all except one little teapot. Entranced by the music, and no doubt not interested in being a teapot again, Cherith was dancing. Looking very much like a young colt learning to walk, Cherith bent and swayed to the music.

By this time, I knew they were laughing at my daughter.

Mercifully, the presentation was short, and it was time to leave. Each child curtsied to the dancing teacher and left with her proud mother.

Cherith was third in line. I closed my eyes and breathed a prayer. Cherith's curtsy was indescribable—a most complicated attitude of akimbo elbows and bent knees. Then the inevitable happened. She fell down!

I grabbed her hand and fled. I am grateful Cherith was totally oblivious to my reaction. As I rushed her into the car, she said, "Did you see me dancing, Mommy? Wasn't I beautiful?"

Dance to My Own Song

I am still totally ashamed to admit what happened. Cherith never returned to her dancing school. Mommy's pride couldn't take it.

Fortunately, Cherith is a resilient child, who takes life as it comes. She left dancing school as easily as she had begun. I think she was secretly glad that she could dress up in her "loosies" and leotard and dance without the pink slippers done up or her hair tied back in painful ponytails. Happily, she would find some music on the radio and dance around the living room, lost in her own private dream.

To the trained eye, she is not the graceful ballerina she longs to be. But to those who love her, Cherith is beautiful when she dances.

I long to be like Cherith—to dance to my own song, oblivious to what those around me might think. Too often in my life, I have been afraid to dance because I thought that the world might laugh. My pride has kept me from doing what I most wanted to do. I couldn't let myself go and listen to the particular song that the Lord created for me.

If I had my life to live over, I would dance to my own song!

CHAPTER THIRTEEN

"I would ride more merry-go-rounds."

Let's Run Away from Home!

Not long ago we ran away from home—Nathan, Cherith, my mother, our two dogs, and I. We'd had a terrible day: tempers had flared, tears had flowed, and no one liked anyone very much.

In the middle of yet another confrontation, Nathan had suddenly yelled, "I wish I could run away from home!"

"So do I," I retorted.

So the idea was born. We dressed warmly and bundled kids and dogs into the car. "I don't believe this," said Cherith, the skeptic. "You're really just going shopping aren't you?"

"No," I said. "We're all running away from home. We've had an awful day, and now we're going away somewhere."

"But where are we running away to?" persisted Cherith.

"Let's go to High Park," I suggested.

Thirty years before, when I had been a little girl in Toronto, mother and I had often run away to High

Let's Run Away from Home!

Park. It seemed like a perfect place to take this next generation of runaways.

It was a blustery April day, late in the afternoon, and there were few people left in the park when we arrived. Surprisingly, very little had changed. The roads were now paved, but everything else was just as I remembered it.

Gleefully, I led the children and dogs to the small zoo. It, too, hadn't changed. Popcorn vendors stood on every corner, and the same smell of roasted peanuts drifted with the breeze. Only the bad-tempered, mangy camel was missing. We romped and laughed our way down the path, stopping to admire the peacocks and feed the reindeer.

Cherith kept anxiously inquiring if this was all we had to do. In her heart of hearts, she suspected that there must be more to it than just sheer fun. She asked for popcorn and, to her surprise, got a bag, even though it wasn't long until supper. Not to be outdone, Nathan spied the candied apples. Cherith dropped hers, and no one yelled at her to leave it because it was dirty.

"Rinse it under the water fountain," I said. "It's all right."

The dogs were wild, barking at the buffalo and making mad dashes at the squirrels. They, too, seemed to have caught the holiday spirit.

At the end of two hours, we were all home again.

The Daisies Are Still Free

We were restored in body and refreshed in spirit, happily watching Walt Disney on television and munching our fried chicken.

"Let's run away from home again," suggested Nathan.

"How about tomorrow instead of school?" said Cherith with a grin.

"We will do it again," I promised them. "We'll run away from home more often. Next time, we'll go to the playground in the park and ride the merry-go-round."

"You, too, mommy?"

"Yes, me, too," I declared.

Later that evening, thinking over the afternoon, I realized that to run away from home and ride the merry-go-round was the ultimate escape. Merry-go-rounds are the epitome of noncompetitiveness. They serve no purpose, go nowhere. To ride a merry-go-round is to declare to the world that your actions are purposeless and that you have no destination.

In a world that believes we should always be upwardly mobile, moving ahead as we "climb ladders and chase dollars," riding the merry-go-round is an act of cowardice.

When I worked for a large computer corporation, we were constantly told, "It's a tough marketplace out there. You've got to fight to win." The entire business community was considered a giant battlefield on

Let's Run Away from Home!

which wars were won and lost by aggressive salesmanship. The winners were rewarded with more pay, more responsibilities, more promotions, and more battles. The losers were relegated to the merry-go-round, going nowhere and fighting no one.

To voluntarily choose the merry-go-round is to be branded a loser.

I once made a beautiful rag doll for a friend's daughter. The pattern for the old-fashioned doll had a hand-embroidered face, an intricate wool hairstyle, and even separate fingers on the stuffed hands. I enjoyed making the lacy underwear, creating little, lace-up boots, and sewing the frilly dress. The doll was truly lovely when I finished. I hadn't counted the hours of work or the cost of the materials. I had simply enjoyed creating her.

Soon, other mothers were calling me, wanting similar dolls for their daughters. The time and cost were then important, since I had to put a price on my product.

At first, I continued to create each doll individually, but I soon found that it took too much time. So, I started a small production line—cutting out several patterns at once, mass-producing the clothes, using the same hairstyle for each, and painting rather than embroidering the faces.

One evening, as I sat up late sewing up the umpteenth pair of boots, I realized that I was not enjoying

The Daisies Are Still Free

myself. The dolls had become a chore. Not only that, the dolls themselves were no longer beautiful in their unique individuality.

I was certainly profiting from them, but I had lost my creative enjoyment in each one. I had been lured by the promise of bigger and better, greater and more. I had stepped off the merry-go-round and into the marketplace.

I made no more dolls for pure profit or production. Now, I only make one when there is some special child I wish to give her to.

If I had my life to live over, I would choose to ride the merry-go-round. Yes, I would run away from home more often and ride the merry-go-round.

CHAPTER FOURTEEN

"I would pick more daisies."

The Daisies Are Still Free

Come with me and pick some daisies.

Imagine a winding dirt road deep in the country. It is a warm afternoon in early summer. You are walking down the road barefoot. Feel the warm dust curling up between your toes; smell it in your nostrils. The sun feels hot on your shoulders, but there is a small breeze blowing the hair off your brow. The air is sweet with the scent of sun-warmed earth, clover in the ditches, fresh grass, and honeysuckle blossoms. You can hear a cricket singing and from a small coppice in the distance comes the song of an oriole. Above you, the sky is like an inverted, blue bowl, clear and cloudless, marked only by a flock of small birds darting to the woods.

As you walk upon the road, you notice that there is a large field opening up on one side of you. The breeze ripples the grasses, and you see among them hundreds and hundreds of nodding daisies.

Suddenly, you are aware of a stong desire to pick the daisies. You stop and stand by the side of the

The Daisies Are Still Free

road, and as you look across at the daisies, you remember....

Moments you have missed because you were afraid to make a mistake....

Times when you've been tense, uptight, and unable to relax and enjoy the abundant life....

Times when you've been afraid to be silly, to laugh, to romp, to play....

Dreams that you've missed because you were afraid to take a chance....

Beautiful moutains you've never climbed; inviting roads you've never traveled; flowing rivers you've never crossed....

Times when you've wanted to follow the Spirit's leading, but you've been sensible instead....

Moments upon moments you've missed because you were looking beyond them....

Things you have insisted on carrying with you everywhere; things you've packed for protection....

Places you have never touched because you left your shoes on....

Dances you have never danced....

Merry-go-rounds you have never ridden.

Look at the daisies again.

Is there a fence between you and the daisy field? Jesus is opening a hidden gate for you.

Is there a high wall in front of you? Jesus will lift you over it.

The Daisies Are Still Free

Is there a wide ditch filled with water? Jesus will build a bridge for you.

Are there people standing between you and the daisies? Jesus will take your hand and lead you through them.

Are you unable to move? Jesus will carry you to the daisies.

Are you afraid to touch the daisies? Jesus will pick them and hand them to you. They are yours.

The daisies are still free.